AGENTS FOR SALE OF MAPS.

Place.	Name of Agent.	Address.
England ...	Mr. Edward Stanford ...	Nos. 12, 13 and 14, Long Acre, London, S. E.
Calcutta ...	(1) The Officer in Charge Map Record and Issue Office.	No. 13, Wood Street, Calcutta.
	(2) Messrs. Thacker, Spink & Co. ...	Nos. 5 & 6, Government Place, North.
	(3) Messrs. Newman & Co. ...	No. 4, Dalhousie Square.
	(4) The Secretary, School Book Society	No. 309, Bow Bazar Street.
	(5) M. Gulab Singh & Sons ...	No. 76, Lower Circular Road.
Bombay ...	(1) Messrs. Thacker & Co. ... (2) D. B. Taraporevala Sons & Co. ...	Bombay.
Rangoon ...	Messrs. Myles, Standish & Co. ...	Rangoon.
Srinagar ...	Mrs. C. Winter	The Picture-Gallery, Srinagar.
Poona ...	Superintendent, Government Photo-zincographic Department.	Poona.
Madras ...	Messrs. Higginbotham & Co. ...	Madras.
Mussooree ...	Proprietor, Mafasilite Printing Works ...	Mussooree.
Lahore ...	Rai Sahib Munshi Gulab Singh and Sons, Government Publishers and Booksellers.	Lahore.
Simla ...	Messrs. Thacker, Spink & Co. ...	Simla.

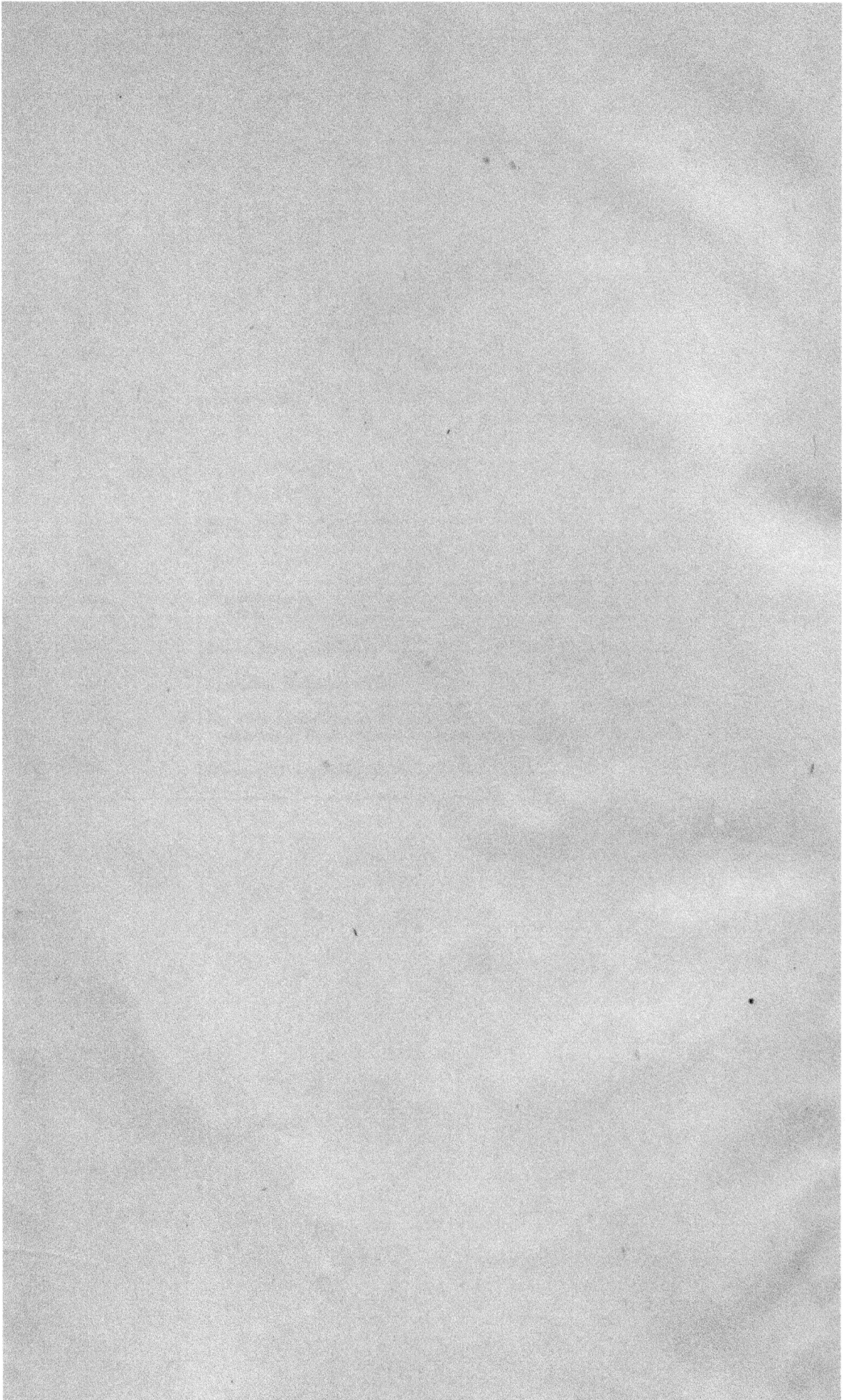

Survey of India.

THE REPRODUCTION

OF

MAPS, PLANS, PHOTOGRAPHS, DIAGRAMS,

AND

LINE ILLUSTRATIONS

BY THE

SURVEY OF INDIA

FOR OTHER DEPARTMENTS.

PREPARED UNDER THE DIRECTION OF

COLONEL S. G. BURRARD, C.S.I., R.E., F.R.S.,

SURVEYOR GENERAL OF INDIA.

CALCUTTA.

1914.

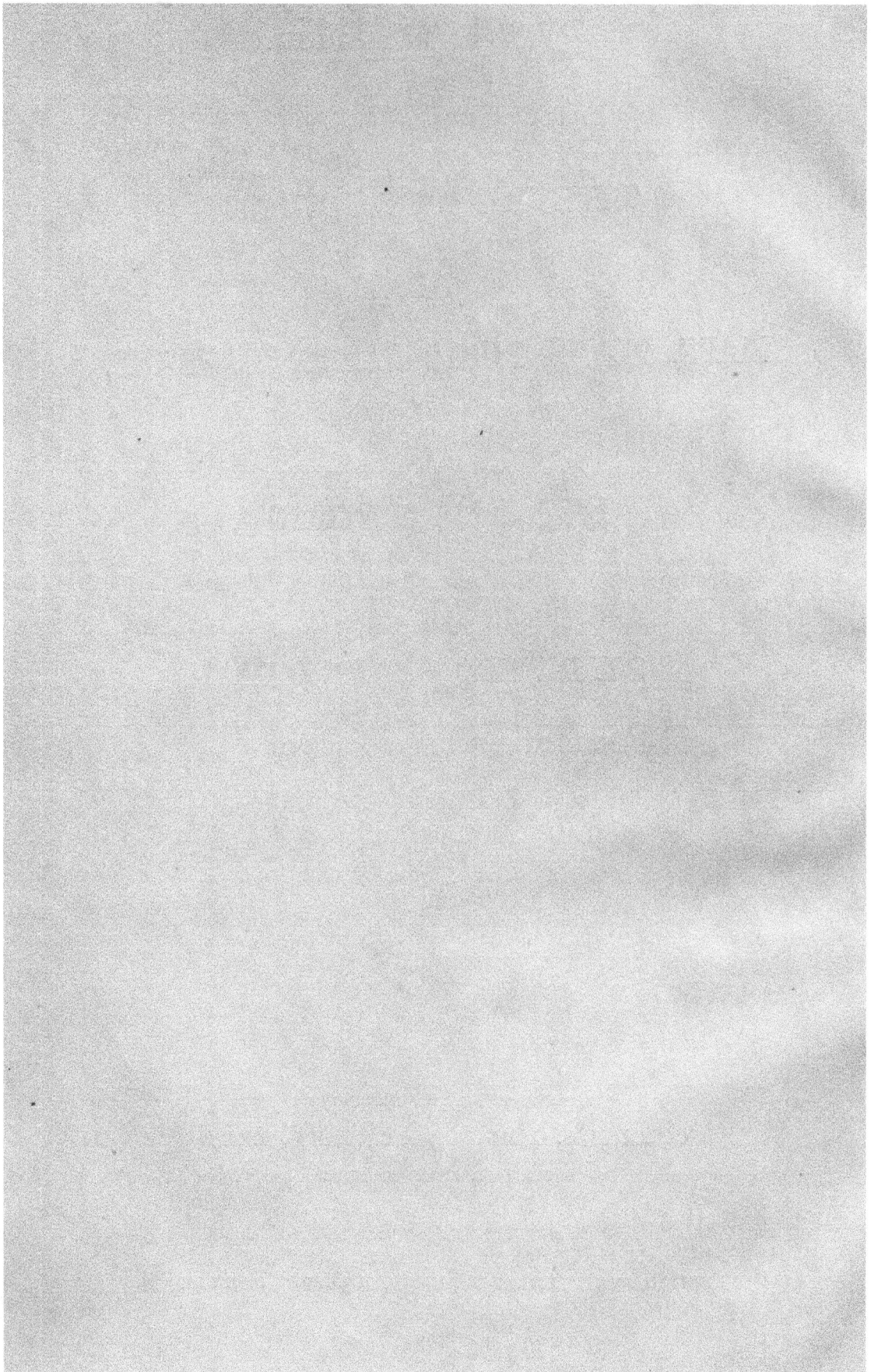

PREFACE.

THE instructions contained in the following pages are based on notes made by Captains Trenchard, Gwyn and Hamilton who have been in charge of the Photo.-Litho. Office, and by the Managers of the Photo. and Litho. branches of the Office,—Messrs. Taylor and Vandyke, with a view to assist officers, other than those of the Survey of India, who may wish to have maps, plans or illustrations reproduced for public purposes by the Survey of India. Such officers require information regarding the conditions on which their work can be undertaken, the different processes available, those most suited for their particular purposes, and the manner in which their drawings should be prepared. Every endeavour has been made to supply this information clearly and if the instructions are carefully followed, much labour, time and expense will be saved to Government.

The Superintendent, Map Publication, Survey of India, will be glad to advise officers regarding the preparation and reproduction of their maps, plans, illustrations, &c., when asked to do so.

This compilation and the selection of the illustrations is due to Captain Sackville Hamilton, R.E., the present Officer-in-charge.

JANUARY 1914,
SURVEY OF INDIA OFFICES,
13, WOOD STREET,
CALCUTTA.

W. M. COLDSTREAM, *Major, R.E.,*
Superintendent, Map Publication.

CONTENTS.

APPENDIX.

Section I.

*Conditions under which work is undertaken by the Survey of India
for Officers of other departments.*

1. The Superintendent, Map Publication is authorised by the Surveyor General of India to undertake the reproduction of maps and other drawings, and of photographs, for other departments of the public services, and for municipalities, railways, port trust and similar public bodies, provided the drawings, &c., are supplied in a form suitable for reproduction by a photographic process.

2. The Surveyor General reserves the right to refuse any work which can not be undertaken without delaying the work of his own department. It is hoped, however, that it will seldom be necessary to refuse work which has been drawn correctly so that it can be reproduced by a photographic process.

3. Although every effort is made to deal expeditiously with work undertaken for other departments, such work is only accepted on the condition that it does not delay work specially ordered by the Government of India or departmental work.

4. Except in very special cases, the preparation of drawings by the Survey of India is confined to departmental work, and to such special drawings as it may be ordered to prepare by the Government of India.

5. The normal scales of Indian maps are :—

$$1 \text{ Mile} = 1 \text{ inch } \left(\tfrac{1}{63,360}\right).$$

$$4 \text{ Miles} = 1 \text{ inch } \left(\tfrac{1}{253,440}\right).$$

$$*16 \text{ Miles} = 1 \text{ inch } \left(\tfrac{1}{1,000,000}\right).$$

$$32 \text{ Miles} = 1 \text{ inch } \left(\tfrac{1}{2,027,520}\right) \text{ A general map in 12 sheets.}$$

$$64 \text{ Miles} = 1 \text{ inch } \left(\tfrac{1}{4,055,040}\right) \quad ,, \quad ,, \quad 4 \ ,,$$

$$128 \text{ Miles} = 1 \text{ inch } \left(\tfrac{1}{8,110,080}\right) \quad ,, \quad ,, \quad 1 \ ,,$$

* This is approximately the scale, exactly it is 15·7823 miles = 1 inch or 16 miles = 1·014 inches.

6. A catalogue of the Survey of India maps available and copies of maps on these scales for almost any part of India which are prepared and printed as the normal work of the Map Publication Offices are obtainable on indent, (*vide* page 42, Appendix *ii*), from the Map Record and Issue Office, 13, Wood Street, Calcutta, and through agencies in large towns. Special maps for other departments, or for public bodies, can sometimes be prepared from them without the preparation of fresh drawings. See page 3, Section II.

7. Military Staff Officers who wish to make use of the Survey of India Maps for the preparations of special maps should refer to Indian Army Order No. 506 of 1909. (See Appendix *i*).

8. Payment for work for Government purposes will be made by book debit; while that for municipalities, railways, &c., will be paid for in cash.

The charges are those at present in force and are liable to slight variations.

SECTION II.

Hints regarding the preparation of maps, plans, sketches, &c., for the illustration of reports and other pamphlets.

1. *Maps.*—It should often be unnecessary to prepare a special map to illustrate an official report. The normal Survey of India sheets are obtainable, and all that may be necessary is to include one of them in the report.

2. The ordinary Survey of India maps may not, however, contain all the special information required to illustrate a report on some particular subject and a special map may be necessary. In such cases the author can arrange to have the special map drawn for reproduction by one of the processes described in Section IV of this pamphlet and should read carefully the instructions in that Section and on page 5 before he puts the drawing in hand, or he may enquire from the Superintendent, Map Publication whether it would be practicable to prepare a special edition of an existing Survey of India Map covering the area with which he is concerned, to show such special information as may be necessary.

3. For small skeleton sketch maps and plans, or other line illustrations which are to be printed as insets in the letter press of the report, a drawing as described under 'line blocks' on page 33 should be prepared. Such illustrations, if they are to be printed with the letter press, can only be printed in black; when the line block has been prepared it should be sent to the office or firm which is to print the report.

4. Sketch maps, plans, diagrams and other line illustrations that are not to appear as insets in the letter press of the report, but as separate plates, should be drawn or traced for heliozincography or the Vandyke process. The instructions contained on page 5 and in pages 7—17, Section IV should be carefully read before the drawing is put in hand.

5. For all ordinary reports, especially if they are of merely ephemeral interest, the sketches, plans, and other line illustrations should be reproduced by the Vandyke process. (See pages 13—17.)

6. If reproductions of photographs are required to illustrate a report, the negatives rather than photographic prints should be sent for reproduction or reduction. In all ordinary cases the half-tone block process (section IV-6) will be used. For reports that are important or of permanent interest or when a high degree of artistic excellence is aimed at, it may be worth while to use the photogravure process for the frontispiece and some of the more important plates. But photogravure is a slow and expensive process. If the subject of an illustration is a comparatively small article, it is better to send the article itself to the Survey of India Offices, rather than a negative or print, as all facilities in the way of apparatus, colour sensitised plates, compensating light filters, &c., are available at Calcutta for obtaining the best possible negative.

7. Panoramic views are frequent accompaniments to reports; if in black line they reproduce well by heliozincography, and provided the lettering is sufficiently large, they are improved by reduction. If they are in shade and line combined very fair results can be obtained by the half-tone process.

8. Graphic charts to illustrate variations, *e.g.*, the rise and fall of prices or the increase and decrease of population, are coming more and more into use for returns and reports on nearly every subject. If such returns have to be periodically prepared a plate containing the permanent portion of the diagram can be kept standing, and the Superintendent, Map Publication will be glad to advise as to the easiest way of periodically inserting and publishing the variable information.

9. The preparation of a map may require more time than the writing of the report it is intended to illustrate, and the illustrations for a report should, therefore, if possible, be put in hand not later than the preparation of the report itself. This is not generally realised and too frequently an author does not consider the preparation of his maps and other illustrations until he has drafted his report, or even sent it to press, with the almost inevitable consequence of delay in publication.

10. The Superintendent, Map Publication, Survey of India, 13, Wood Street, Calcutta, will be glad to advise officers as to the best method of preparing their maps and plans for reproduction.

Section III.

General rules to be observed in the preparation of drawings, &c.,
for reproduction.

The following rules are very important; they apply to the preparation of drawings for reproduction by any photographic process:—

1.   All drawing and lettering must be in **BLACK, OPAQUE, INDIAN INK.**   The lines may be fine, but they should be smooth and not broken.   It should be borne in mind that all defects in the drawings will appear in the printed copies.   The paper should be white or bluish, not yellowish.

ORIGINALS MUST NOT BE FOLDED OR CREASED.

SIGNATURES to maps and plans, &c., should be in black Indian Ink, if they are intended to be reproduced; ordinary writing ink does not reproduce well.

2.   **NO COLOUR** of any sort should be applied to a drawing or trace for photography.

3.   **THE DRAWING MUST BE CORRECT AND COMPLETE** : it should be very carefully examined *before* it is sent for reproduction, and any errors discovered should be corrected on the drawing or trace exactly as they are intended to appear in the printed copies.

In the heliozincographic process only minor corrections will be made at proof stage.

In the Vandyke process **CORRECTIONS ARE NOT UNDERTAKEN** and proofs are not usually supplied.   If corrections are necessary the original must be corrected and re-Vandyked.

With the half-tone process no corrections can be made.

With the line block process corrections are difficult and occasionally impossible.

The greatest care should also be taken that where type matter has to be set up with reports, illustrations or maps that the original specimen is correct in the first instance.   The alteration of one word may mean that the whole has to be re-composed and it will be readily understood that the importance of the correctness of the originals and first instructions cannot be over-estimated.

4.   Each additional colour in which a map or other illustration is printed adds materially to the cost and labour of reproduction.   Colour printing should be avoided as far as possible, and when it is necessary the number of colours should be the minimum that will suffice

5.   Detailed instructions for the preparation of originals are given separately for each process in Section IV.

SECTION IV.

The following is a tabular statement of the processes of reproduction giving the specimen plates used for each descriptive of the purposes for which each is suitable. All information required is given and each process is illustrated separately :—

No.	Process.	Page.	Specimen Plates.	Purposes for which the process is suitable.
1	Heliozincography ...		Illustration describing process. Extract from 1″ standard sheet in colours. Specimen of ½″ work in black.	The reproduction of maps, charts, diagrams and line illustrations.
2	The Vandyke process		Illustration shewing method of production in colours. Specimen page in black shewing :— A map. A mechanical drawing.	The reproduction of maps, charts, diagrams and line illustrations where the highest quality of impression is not essential. Copies can only be reproduced on the same scale as the original.
3	Lithography ..		*Nil.* Not available for extra-departmental work.	Maps and diagrams.
4	Engraving on copper		*Nil.* Not available for extra-departmental work except in very special cases.	Maps, line illustrations, and diagrams, Commissions, addresses and certificates.
5	Photogravure ...		Portraiture ... A Seascape. Architectural.	The reproduction of portraits and illustrations.
6	Half-tone blocks ...		Scientific (2 plates) ... A Seascape. A Landscape.	Illustrations or portraits in half-tone. The blocks can be set up with type and are printed in a letter press machine.
7	Line blocks ...		A small map ... Two diagrams.	Small maps, line illustrations or diagrams, especially if a large number of copies are required. The blocks can be set up with type and are printed in a letter-press machine.

1.—HELIOZINCOGRAPHY.

———:o:———

(The reproduction of Maps, Charts, Diagrams and Line Illustrations).

————

SPECIMEN PLATES :—

Illustration describing process.

Extract from 1″ standard sheet in colours.

Specimen of ½″ work in black.

1 - HELIOZINCOGRAPHY.

1. *The nature of the originals.*—The "original" drawings for the helio-zincographic process should be prepared in one of the three forms named below :—

(*i*)   A line drawing in **BLACK** on white or bluish paper, or on Bristol Board.

(*ii*)   A good tracing or a drawing in **BLACK** on tracing cloth.

(*iii*)   A clear sharp line impression, printed by any process on white or bluish paper.

2. *General instructions for preparation of the originals additional to the general rules contained in Section III.*—Drawings for the photozincographic process should, if possible, be drawn on a scale larger than that of the printed copies asked for, so that advantage may be taken of photographic reduction which reduces minor defects in drawing and lettering, and gives sharper and cleaner results than reproduction to scale.

A suitable scale for heliozincography is one and a half times that required for the printed copies; if the best results irrespective of the inconvenience of the size of the original drawing are aimed at, the scale of the drawing may be twice that of the printed copies.

In all cases where drawings are to be reduced care must be taken to make the lettering and figures sufficiently large to stand the required reduction.

SIGNATURES should be in black Indian Ink; ordinary writing ink does not reproduce.

If expense and time are not of first importance an excellent plan is to rough draft the map or diagram to the scale on which the copies are required. The rough draft can then be enlarged in the Map Publication Office and a light blue print on drawing paper supplied to the draftsman to ink up as an original fair drawing; a good quality indian ink freshly made up or process black should be used.

3. *Reproduction in colours.*—This method is particularly useful if the work is to be printed in colours, because separate blue prints, one for each colour, can be pulled from the same plate to "register" together. As light blue does not reproduce photographically the work can be inked up as finely as may be required, and the blue lines on the print may be neglected. Under this method a separate drawing is required for the black and for each colour. These must be in black irrespective of the colour to which they refer and must "register" exactly with each other, the greatest care being taken that the corner registration marks (see plate, page 10) are correctly placed. Each of them must shew nothing but the lettering and drawing to be printed in the particular colour to which it refers. It must, however, be borne in mind that with this method it is extremely difficult to obtain correct register and that the more usual method with this process is the alternative one given below.

4. This alternative method is to draw the whole of the lettering and detail, irrespective of the colour in which it is to be printed on one "original" in black and a pattern should then be supplied either with the drawing or on a preliminary grey proof indicating the colours in which it is to be reproduced. With either method flat tints or washes of colour can be printed as well as colours in line if they are indicated on a separate colour pattern. No colour must appear on the originals.

The specimen illustrative of the process (method 2) shows contours. It should be remembered that only very open contours can be shewn on the same original as the detail as they make retouching extremely difficult and that where they are close a completely separate contour original is required. The reproduction of contours on maps is not ordinarily undertaken for departments other than those of the Survey of India.

This alternative method is the ordinary process used in the production of the Survey of India maps. Heliozincography is more expensive and slower than the Vandyke process, but the results are superior.

The quality of the results depends on that of the originals and the degree of reduction employed.

Each additional colour in which a map or diagram is printed adds considerably to the cost.

5. *Corrections.*—Only minor corrections can be carried out at proof stage; all corrections, however small, cause considerable inconvenience, expense, and delay. **THE ORIGINALS SHOULD BE CORRECT AND COMPLETE IN THE FIRST INSTANCE.**

6. *Printing paper.*—The maximum size of map that can be printed by this method is 43″ × 29″; details as to size, cost, &c. of paper are given in Section V.

The papers most suitable for heliozincography are listed together at the beginning of Section V. Specimens of paper are given as per the illustrations annexed.

7. *Cost.*—The charges for heliozincographic work are as given on Section VI.

A specimen estimate is given below for—

	Rs.	As.	P.
1,100 copies of a map, 21″ × 19″ in black and 4 colours—			
5 Negatives, 24″ × 22″, @ Rs. 8-8-0 each ...	42	8	0
Retouching and cutting (approximate) ...	10	0	0
5 Imperial size Helios., @ Rs. 4-0-0 each (preparation of plate from a negative) ...	20	0	0
Proving 5 Imperial Helios., @ Rs. 4-0-0 each ...	20	0	0
Printing 1,100 copies (5 printings)	164	8	0
Paper (67 ℔s rag-litho.)	50	0	0
TOTAL Rs. ...	307	0	0

The charges given in Section VI for printing are for one colour only. For maps in more than one colour, the rates charged for each extra printing will be one rupee higher than those given in the table for each hundred of the first thousand and eight annas extra for each subsequent hundred.

8. *Custody of plates.*—Plates can be kept standing at a charge of Rs. 10-0-0 each, but the Survey of India does not hold itself responsible for their deterioration; ordinarily plates should keep for years. Plates are cleaned off unless a definite request is made for their retention.

ILLUSTRATIONS DESCRIPTIVE OF THE HELIOZINCOGRAPHIC PROCESS.

THESE ILLUSTRATIONS ARE PRINTED ON RAG LITHO. PAPER.

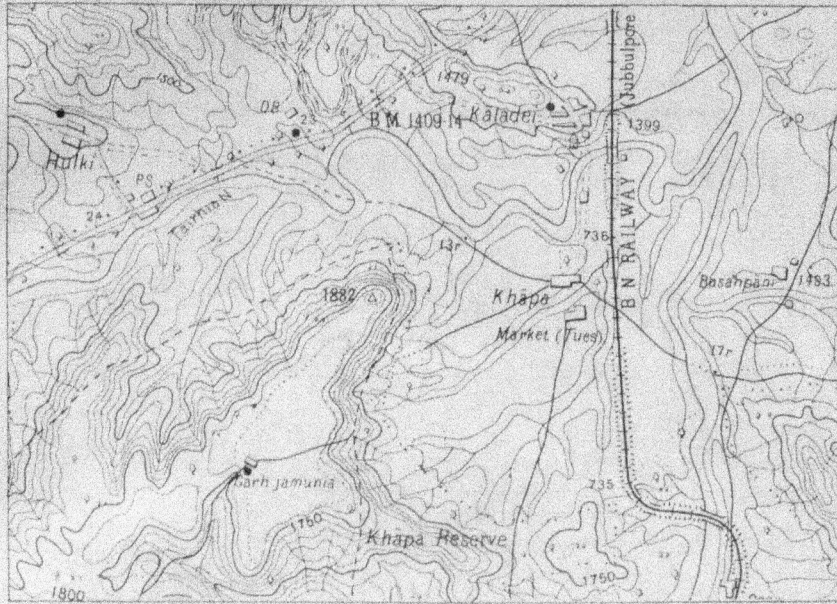

The original Drawing.

The grey proof, on which the Indenting
Party should indicate the colours
for the final map.

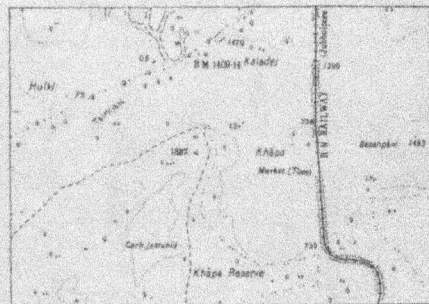

The Black Plate.

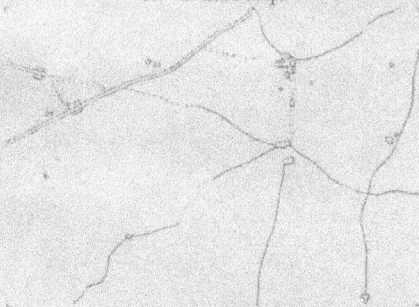

The Red Plate.

The Blue Plate.

The Hill Plate

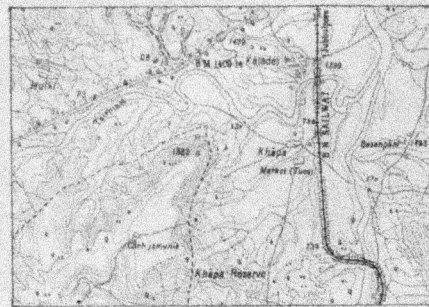

The Final Map.

EXTRACT FROM A ONE INCH STANDARD SHEET IN COLOURS BY THE
HELIOZINCOGRAPHIC PROCESS.

THIS MAP IS PRINTED ON RAG-LITHO. PAPER.

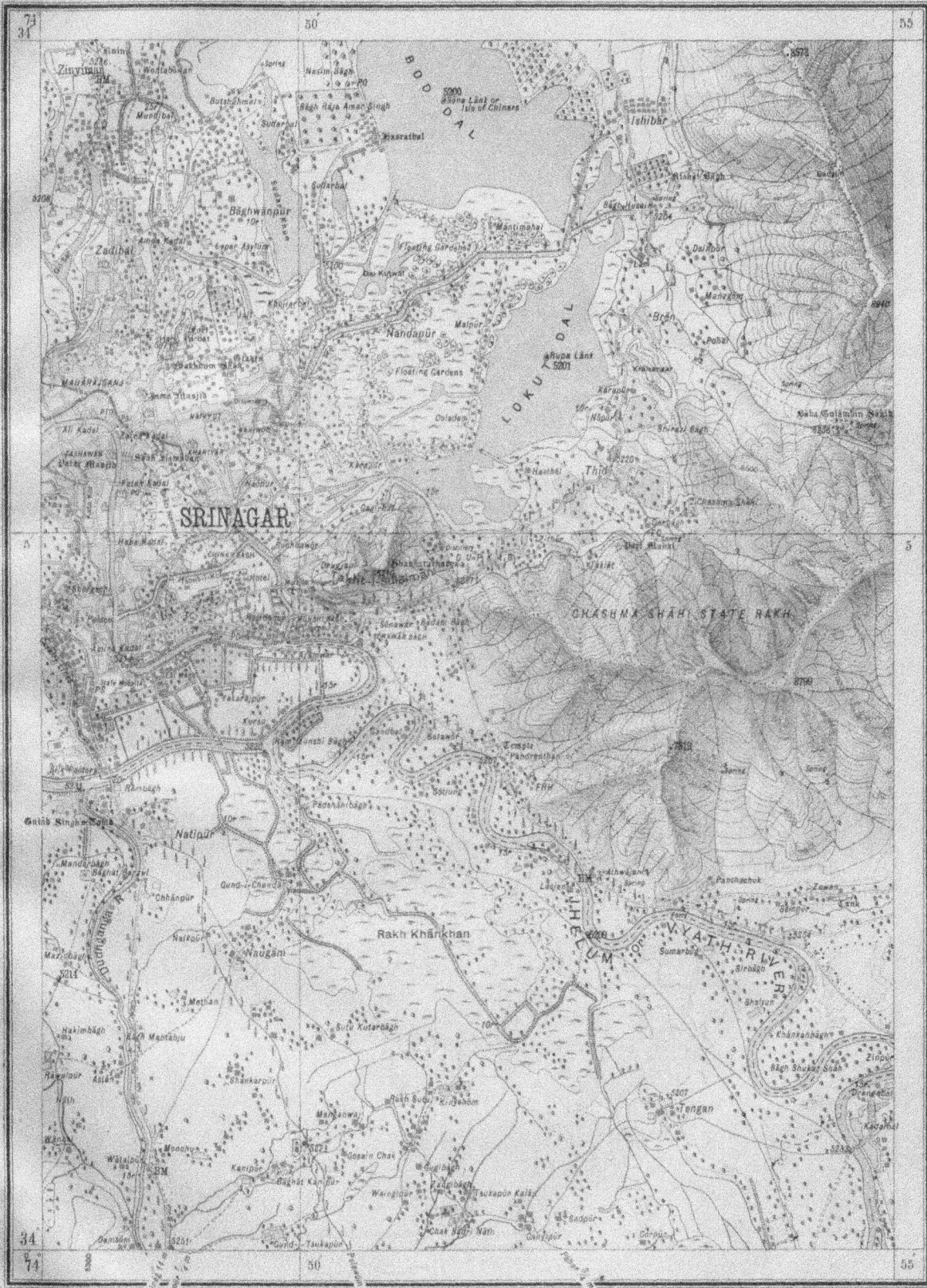

Scale 1 Inch to a Mile, or 1:63,360.

Furlongs 8 6 4 2 0   1   2   3 Miles

SPECIMEN OF HALF-INCH HELIOZINCOGRAPHIC WORK IN BLACK.

THIS MAP IS PRINTED ON RAG-LITHO. PAPER.

No. 46 $\frac{F}{2}$

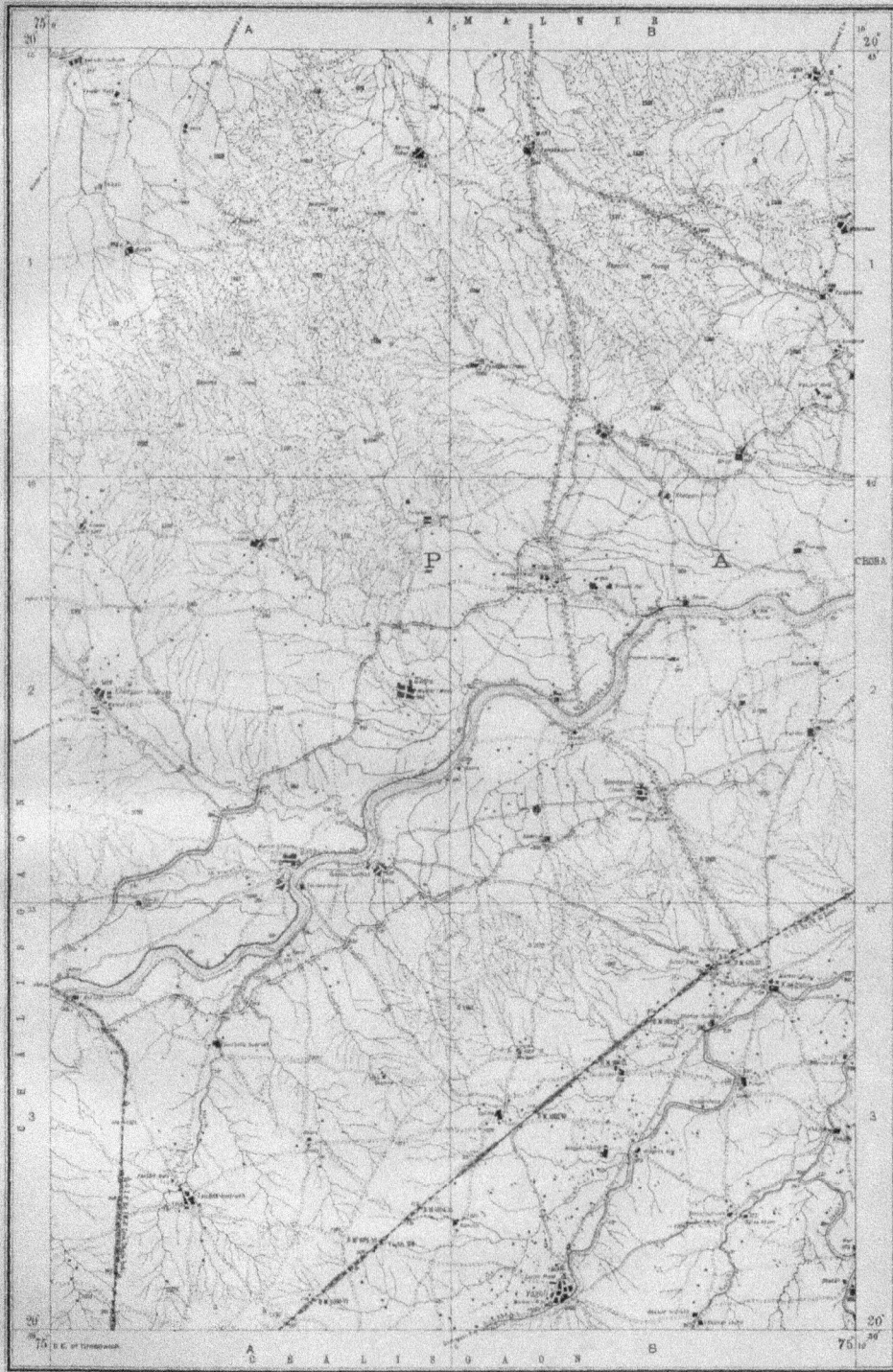

2.—THE VANDYKE PROCESS.

————:o:————

(The Reproduction of Maps, Charts, Diagrams, and Line Illustrations where the highest quality of impression is not essential).

————————

SPECIMEN PLATES:—Illustration shewing method of production in colours.
Specimen page in black shewing:—

A map.

A mechanical drawing.

2.—THE VANDYKE PROCESS.

1. *The nature of the originals.*—The original drawings for the Vandyke process should be prepared in one of the two forms named below :—

> (*i*) A good tracing or drawing in **BLACK** on tracing *cloth.*
>
> (*ii*) **BLACK** tracings or drawings on any semi-transparent white or bluish smooth material. Thin white printing paper is suitable; tracing paper is less so.

2. *General instructions for preparation of the originals additional to the general rules contained in Section III.*—The best original for the Vandyke process is a perfectly drawn tracing on blue tracing cloth. Perfectly drawn means that every line must be absolutely black and opaque : a good test is to hold the tracing up against a very strong light and carefully examine it for any sign of greyness or transparency in the line. If found grey or broken it should be returned to the draughtsman for re-inking.

Drawings on paper will also give good results. A smooth wove paper preferably of a bluish shade should be used. Even more care must be taken in drawing on paper as owing to its greater opacity the lines will look blacker than they really are.

Yellow tracing paper or cloth is quite unsuitable and should never be used.

A good quality Indian ink freshly made up or "Process Black" should be used. When drawing on tracing cloth a slight addition of ox-gall will make the Indian ink "take" better. Heavy block letters or border lines should be gone over twice.

SIGNATURES should be in black Indian Ink; ordinary writing ink does not reproduce.

3. *Scale of the originals.*—Reduction or enlargement is not possible if the Vandyke process is used. The maximum size of the original is therefore limited to $43'' \times 29''$.

4. *Reproduction in colours.*—An excellent plan is to rough draft the map or diagram on drawing paper to the scale on which the copies are required. This can then be pinned down on to a drawing board, care being taken to see that the position of the rough draft is not permitted to move, and separate fair drawings on tracing cloth can be made, one for black and for each colour.

These drawings must be in black irrespective of the colour they refer to and must 'register' exactly with each other. Each of them must show nothing but the lettering and drawing to be printed in the particular colour it refers to.

Flat tints or washes of colour can be printed if they are indicated on a separate colour pattern.

No colour must appear on the originals.

This is a cheap and rapid process particularly suitable for rough diagrams, maps, plans, &c.

The quality if the results depends entirely on that of the original.

Each additional colour in which a job is to be printed adds considerably to the cost.

5. *Corrections.*—**CORRECTIONS ARE NOT UNDERTAKEN** and proofs are not usually supplied; **THE ORIGINAL SHOULD BE CORRECT AND COMPLETE IN THE FIRST INSTANCE.**

6. *Printing paper.*—The maximum size of work that can be printed by this method is $43'' \times 29''$.

Details as to size, cost, &c. of paper are given in Section VI.

Specimens of the papers most suitable for the Vandyke process are given as per the illustrations annexed.

7. *Cost.*—The charges for work done by this process are as given in Section VI.

A specimen estimate is given below for 1,000 copies of a map, size 28″ × 19″, in black only.

	Rs.	A.	P.
One D. Z. plate, Imperial size (30″ × 22″) ...	3	0	0
Proving (30″ × 22″)	4	0	0
Printing 1,000 copies (one printing) ...	23	0	0
Paper (67 lbs rag-litho.) ...	55	0	0
TOTAL Rs. ...	85	0	0

The charges given in Section VI for printing are for one colour only. For maps in more than one colour the rates charged for each extra printing will be one rupee higher than those given in the table for each hundred of the first thousand, and 8 annas extra for each subsequent hundred.

8. Plates can be kept standing at a charge of Rs. 10 each, but the Survey of India does not hold itself responsible for their deterioration; ordinarily plates should keep for years.

Plates are cleaned off unless a definite request is made for their retention.

Note.

It is important that there should be no erasures and no pasting on the original. In both cases a different exposure is required to that which would suit the body of the map. It is often better and cheaper in the end to reproduce originals which fail badly in these respects by heliozincography.

ILLUSTRATION SHEWING METHOD OF REPRODUCTION IN COLOURS BY THE VANDYKE PROCESS.

THIS ILLUSTRATION IS PRINTED ON D.E. PROOF (THICK BANKPOST) PAPER.

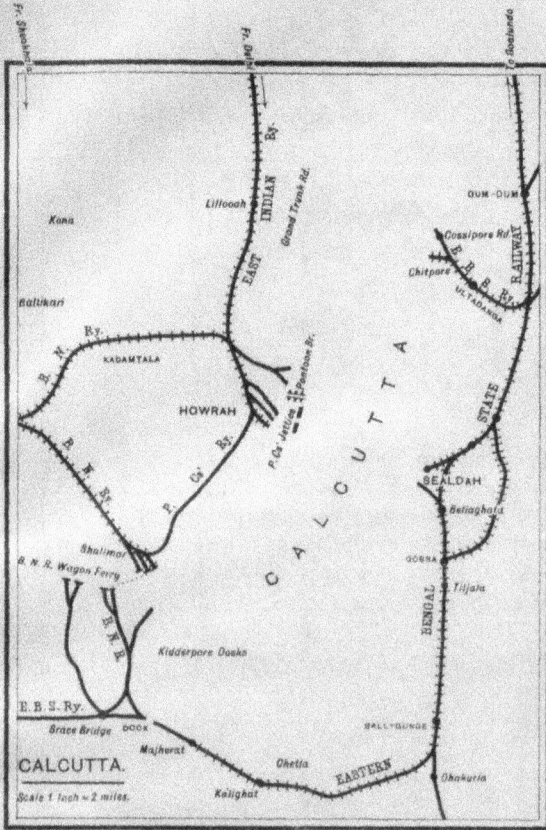

THE BLACK ORIGINAL.

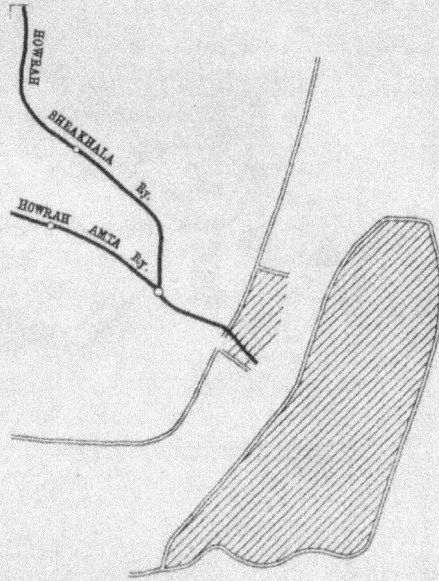

THE RED ORIGINAL.

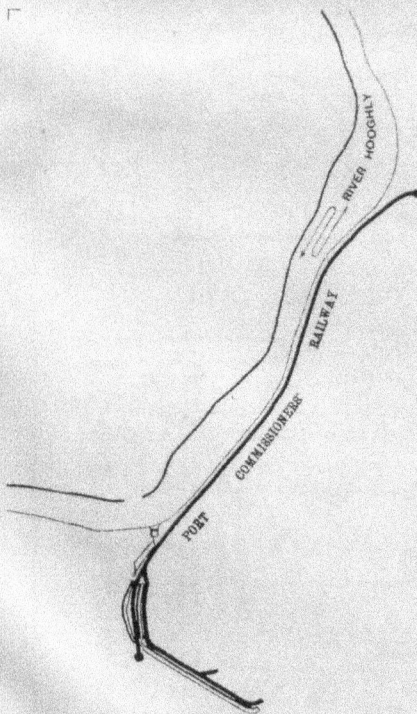

THE BLUE ORIGINAL.

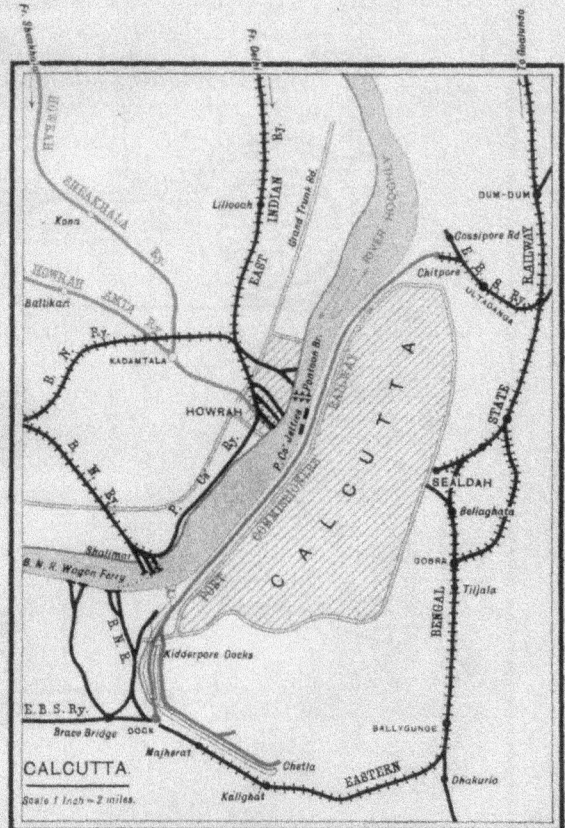

COMPLETE MAP IN THREE COLOURS.

SPECIMEN PAGE IN BLACK BY THE VANDYKE PROCESS.

THESE ILLUSTRATIONS ARE PRINTED ON D. I. LITHO., 110 LBS. PAPER.

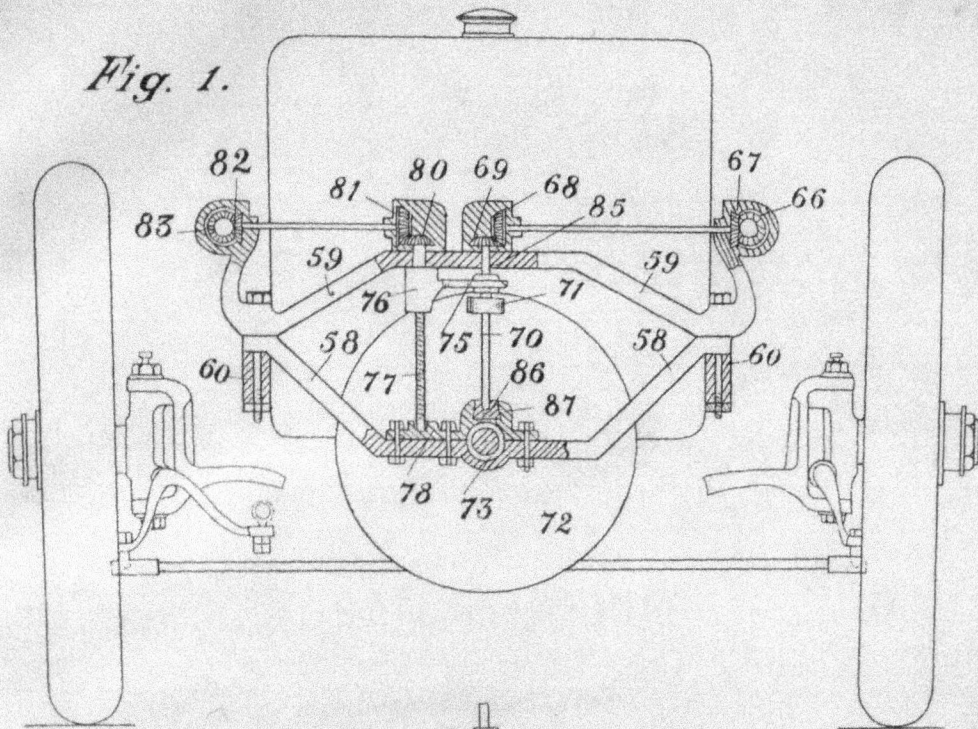

Fig. 1.

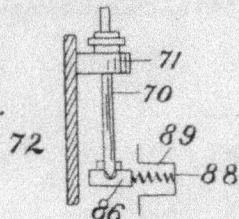

Fig 2.

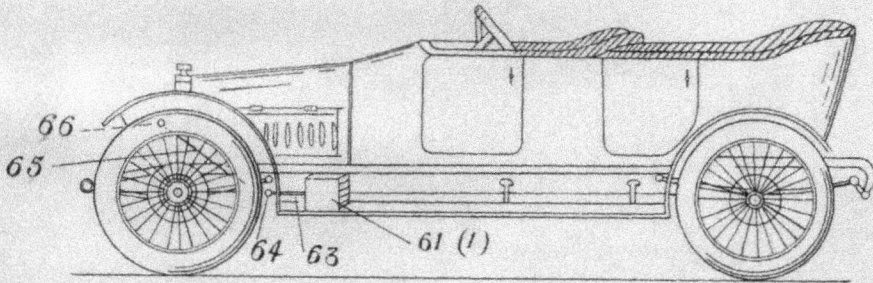

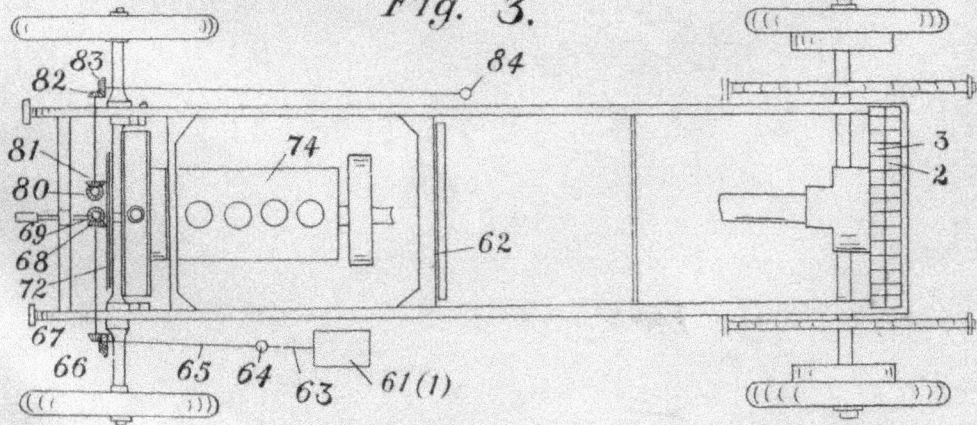

Fig. 3.

3.—LITHOGRAPHY.

———:o:———

(Maps and Diagrams).

Not usually available for extra-departmental work.

3.—LITHOGRAPHY.

1. *The nature of the originals.*—As the map or diagram has to be redrawn on stone, or on transfer paper for transfer to stone, merely a correct and intelligible pattern is required.

This process is slow and is more suitable for small than for large scale maps. It is practically confined to the production of certain Survey of India maps.

2. *Reproduction in colours.*—Copies can be printed in colours, a separate stone being drawn for each colour.

Each separate colour adds very considerably to the cost.

3. *Corrections.*—Corrections can be carried out at proof stage. Each correction required adds largely both to the time required and to the cost of the work.

4. *Printing paper.*—The maximum size of work that can be printed by this method is $43'' \times 29''$; details as to size, cost, &c. of paper are given in Section V. The papers suitable for lithography are similar to those used for the heliographic and Vandyke processes.

5. *Cost.*—The charges for lithographic work are as given in Section VI; no rates can be laid down for drawing work but estimates can always be given when required.

The charges given for printing are for one colour only. For maps in more than one colour, the rates charged for each extra printing will be one rupee higher than those given in the table for each hundred of the first thousand, and eight annas extra for each subsequent hundred.

6. *Custody of stones.*—Stones of extra-departmental work are not kept except in very special cases.

4.—ENGRAVING ON COPPER.

———:o:———

(Maps and Diagrams, Line Illustrations, Commissions,
Addresses and Certificates).

———————

Not usually available for extra-departmental work.

4.—ENGRAVING ON COPPER.

1. *The nature of the originals.*—As the work to be reproduced has to be engraved on copper, merely a correct and intelligible pattern is required.

This process yields the highest quality of map reproduction. It is, however, very slow and extremely expensive and is more suitable for small than for large scale maps.

It is confined to the production of certain classes of Survey of India maps.

2. *Reproduction in colours.*—Copies can be printed in colours, a separate plate being engraved for each colour. Each separate colour adds very considerably to the cost.

3. *Corrections.*—Corrections can be carried out but cause very considerable inconvenience, and a large expenditure of extra labour, time, and money.

4. *Printing paper.*—The maximum size of an engraved copper plate is usually 40″ × 27″ and the paper is limited accordingly. If the map or diagram is first transferred to stone then any paper suitable for lithography can be used for printing. If, however, a few prints are taken direct from the copper plate as is sometimes done, then the paper used will be either rag-litho., Hollingworth, or Whatman's Drawing paper.

5. *Cost.*—No rates can be laid down for engraving work but estimates can always be given when required. The charges for printing are Rs. 75 per 100 for $\frac{1}{4}$ sheet size (20″ × 13$\frac{1}{2}$″) or Rs. 37-8-0 for $\frac{1}{2}$ foolscap size (13$\frac{1}{2}$″ × 10″) irrespective of which of the three papers named above are used.

Charges for larger sizes are in proportion.

6. *Custody of plates.*—Plates when work is undertaken can be kept at a charge of ten rupees per plate.

5.—PHOTOGRAVURE.

———:o:———

(The reproduction of Portraits and Illustrations.)

SPECIMEN PLATES:—Portraiture.
A Seascape.
Architectural.

5.—PHOTOGRAVURE.

1. *The nature of the originals.*—The original for the photogravure process should be one of the following :—

(*i*)—The article or object of art it is proposed to illustrate.

(*ii*)—A good negative.

(*iii*)—A good photographic print on paper such as :—Wellington, Kodak, or Ensign, glossy bromide.

(*iv*)—A brush drawing.

(*v*)—An oil painting.

(*vi*)—A good photographic print on printing out paper.

The above are given in their order of suitability.

2. The maximum size for photogravure is $30'' \times 24''$.

3. It is a monochrome process only. Results are artistic, but it is a slow and expensive process.

4. *Printing paper.*—To produce the best results it is necessary that it should be printed on a heavy plate 240 ℔s paper but good results can also be obtained on Hollingworth, Bankpost or Litho. paper as per that on which the illustrations of photogravure annexed are printed. Details as to size, cost, &c., are given in Section V.

5. The charges for photogravure are as given in Section VI. A specimen estimate for 100 copies of the seascape illustration annexed is given below :—

	Rs.	A.	P.
*Cost of photogravure, 30 inches square, @ Re. 1-0-0 per square inch	30	0	0
Cost of Engraving Title (Approx. av:) ...	10	0	0
„ „ Printing 100 copies	10	12	0
„ „ Paper (D. E. Plate, 240 ℔s)	3	14	0
TOTAL Rs. ...	54	10	0

*Minimum charge for this item is Rs. 25-0-0.

There is no reduction of printing charges for any larger number of copies.

6. *Custody of plates.*—Plates are not kept.

THIS PORTRAIT IS PRINTED ON D. E. 123 LBS. HOLLINGWORTH PAPER.

Photogravure.   Survey of India Offices, Calcutta, 1912.

COLONEL FRANCIS BACON LONGE, C.B., R.E.

Surveyor General, 1904-1911.

THIS ILLUSTRATION IS PRINTED ON D. E. 60 LBS. BANK POST PAPER.

MADRAS HARBOUR.

THIS ILLUSTRATION IS PRINTED ON D. E. 98 LBS. LITHO PAPER.

A JAIN TEMPLE

6.—HALF-TONE BLOCKS.

————:0:————

(Illustrations or Portraits in Half-tone.)

————————

SPECIMEN PLATES :—Scientific (2 plates).

A Seascape.

A Landscape.

6.—HALF-TONE BLOCKS.

1. *The nature of the originals.*—The original for the preparation of a half-tone block should be one of the following :—

    1.—The article or object of art which it is proposed to illustrate.
    2.—A good negative.
    3.—A good photographic print on paper such as :—

        Wellington,
        Kodak, or
        Ensign, glossy bromide.

    4.—A brush drawing.
    5.—An oil painting.
    6.—A good photographic print on printing out paper.

The above are given in their order of suitability.

The original must be complete and correct as alterations and additions can not be made on the blocks.

2. The maximum size for a half-tone block is 20″ × 15″. It is suitable for illustrations or portraits in half-tone and is especially useful when a large number of copies are required, or if the illustration is to be printed as an inset in letter press. The blocks can be set up with type, and are printed in a letter press machine.

It is a cheap and rapid process as compared with photogravure, but results are less artistic.

3. The three-'colour' modification of this process enables coloured originals to be reproduced in colours, within certain limitations. All ordinary half-tone blocks are for printing in monochrome only.

4. *Printing paper.*—Half-tone blocks are printed on art paper as per that of the illustrations of half-tone work annexed. Details as to size, cost, &c., are given in Section V.

5. The charges for half-tone blocks are divided into 3 classes according to the nature of the work and are as given in Section VI.

    Class A is intended for deep-etched work as per specimen annexed.
    Class B „   „   „ ordinary half-tone illustrations.
    Class C „   „   „ rough illustrations.

A specimen estimate for 1,000 copies of the landscape illustration annexed s given below :

	Rs.	A.	P.
Cost of half-tone, 48 square inches, @ 0-12-0 per square inch ("B" class)	36	0	0
Making ready	3	0	0
Typing	1	0	0
Printing 1,000 copies	10	0	0
Paper for 1,000 copies (50 lbs paper)	4	11	6
TOTAL Rs. ...	54	11	6

6. *Custody of blocks.*—The block is the property of the applicant and can be printed at the Survey of India Offices, or by any *good* letter press printer.

HALF-TONE BLOCK CLASS A.

(SCIENTIFIC.)

(Shewing specimen of deep-etched work.)

THIS ILLUSTRATION IS PRINTED ON 90 LBS. ART PAPER.

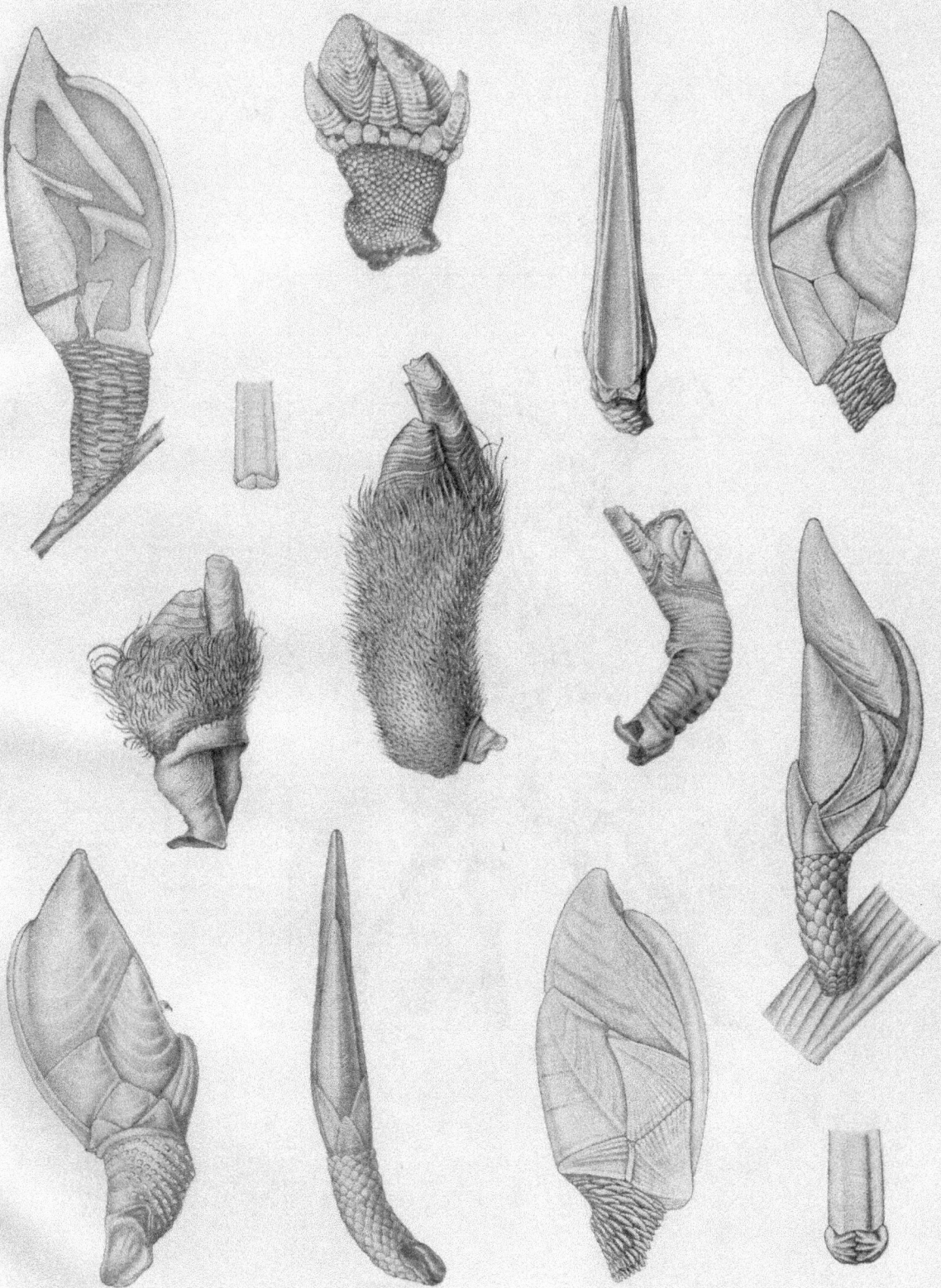

HALF-TONE BLOCK CLASS B.

SCIENTIFIC.

THIS ILLUSTRATION IS PRINTED ON 70 LBS. ART PAPER.

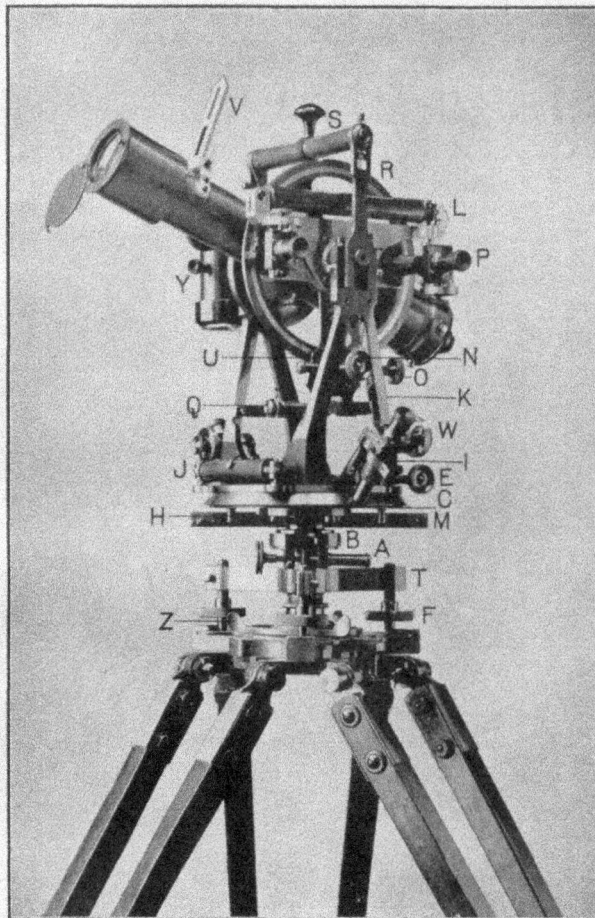

A	Lower tangent screw.
B	Lower clamp.
C	Lower plate.
E	Upper tangent screw.
F	Foot-screw.
G	Upper clamping screw (not visible).
H	Vulcanite knob.
I	Horizontal Microscope.
J	Body level.
K	Standard.
L	Vertical level.
M	Magnetic compass.
N	Vertical clamping screw.
O	Vertical tangent screw.
P	Vertical Microscope.
Q	Vertical clip.
R	Vertical plate.
S	Striding level.
T	Tribrach.
U	Vertical clamp.
V	Sight vane.
W	Micrometer head.
Y	Axis lamp.
Z	Centering clamp.

SMALL MICROMETER TRANSIT THEODOLITE.

HALF-TONE BLOCK, CLASS B.

THIS ILLUSTRATION IS PRINTED ON 50 LBS. ART PAPER.

THE SALWEEN AT TA HSANG LE.

HALF-TONE BLOCK, CLASS B.

THIS ILLUSTRATION IS PRINTED ON DULL ENAMELLED, CHROMO,
250 LBS. PAPER.

MADRAS HARBOUR.

7.—LINE BLOCKS.

————:o:————

(Small maps, Line Illustrations, or Diagrams).

————————

SPECIMEN PLATES:—**A** small map.

Two Diagrams.

7.—LINE BLOCKS.

1. *The nature of the originals.*—The original for the preparation of a line block should be a clear line drawing or print in black on white paper. Drawings for the line block process, should, if possible, be drawn on a scale larger than that of the printed copies asked for, so that advantage may be taken of photographic reduction which reduces minor defects in drawing and lettering and gives sharper and clearer results than reproduction to scale. One-half reduction is suitable. In all cases where drawings are to be reduced care must be taken to make the lettering and figures sufficiently large to stand the required reduction.

The drawing must be correct and complete as alterations and corrections can seldom be made.

2. The maximum size for a line block is $30'' \times 20''$ but it is not economical to use line block above $15'' \times 12''$. Anything over this should be produced by heliozincography.

It is suitable for small maps, line illustrations or diagrams ; especially if a large number of copies are required or which it is required to print as insets in letter press. The blocks can be set up with type, and are printed in a letter press machine.

Ordinary maps, line illustrations and diagrams are more cheaply reproduced by heliozincography or by the Vandyke process.

3. It is a monochrome process and is not ordinarily used for colour work. It can, however, be done provided there is a separate original for each colour. These must be in black irrespective of the colour to which they refer and must "register" exactly with each other. Each of them must shew nothing but the lettering and drawing to be printed in the particular colour to which it refers. A separate line block for each colour can then be prepared from these. The drawings must be correct and complete as alterations and corrections are difficult and sometimes impossible.

4. *Printing paper.*—For the finest work in the line block process, art paper is a necessity for printing purposes, but for ordinary work any paper that is suitable for heliozincography or the Vandyke process can be used. Details as to size, cost, &c., are given in Section V.

5. The charges for line blocks are divided into two classes and are as given in Section VI.

Class A is intended for the finest line work to be printed on art paper.

Class B „ „ „ rough open line work to be printed with type matter on common paper.

A specimen estimate for 1,000 copies of Diagram No. II annexed (A class) is given below—

	Rs.	A.	P.
Cost of line block, 14 sq. inches, @ 0-8-0 per sq. inch	7	0	0
Making ready	3	0	0
Typing	1	0	0
Printing 1,000 copies	7	8	0
Paper (50 lbs Art paper) ...	9	7	0
TOTAL Rs. ...	27	15	0

6. *Custody of line blocks.*—The block is the property of the applicant and can be printed at the Survey of India Offices, or by any *good* letter press printer.

SPECIMEN OF A SMALL MAP BY THE LINE-BLOCK PROCESS.

THIS MAP IS PRINTED ON RAG-LITHO. PAPER.

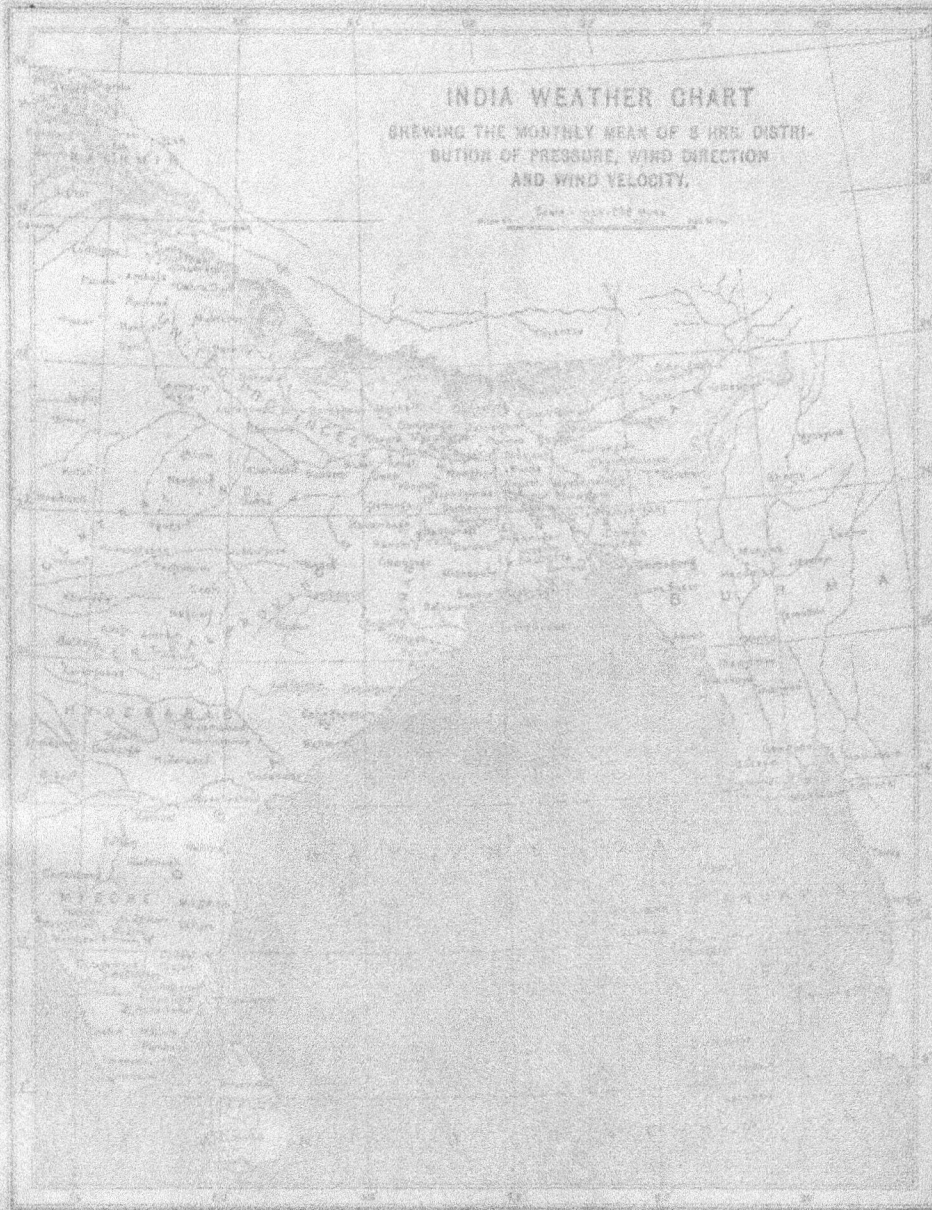

SPECIMEN OF DIFFERENT CLASSES OF ILLUSTRATIVE DIAGRAMS BY THE
LINE BLOCK PROCESS.

THESE DIAGRAMS ARE PRINTED ON 50 LB. ART PAPER.

I

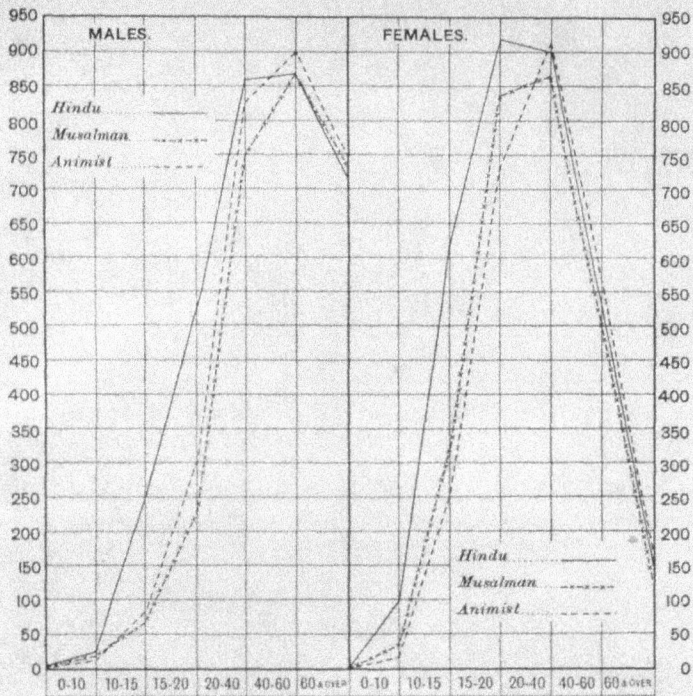

SHEWING AN ORDINARY COMPARATIVE DIAGRAM.

II

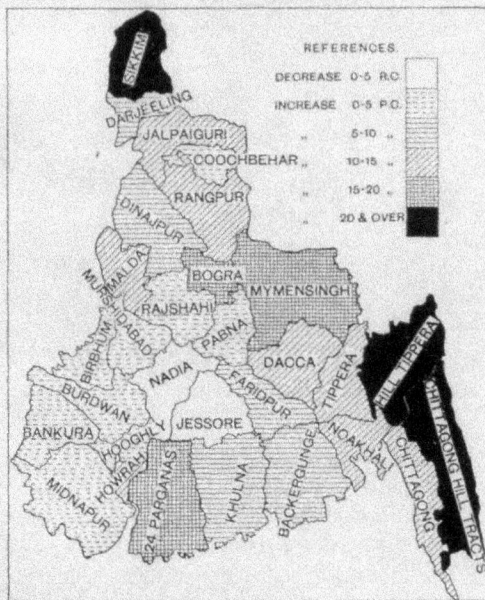

SHEWING THE USE OF CROSS RULINGS OVER DIFFERENT AREAS.

SUMMARY OF FOREGOING INFORMATION.

SUMMARY OF INSTRUCTIONS

Process.	Purposes for which it is suitable.	Nature of "original" suitable for the process.
1. Heliozincography ...	Maps, charts, diagrams, line illustrations ... Maximum size, 43″×29″.	One of the following:— (i) A line drawing in black on white or bluish paper. (ii) A good tracing or a drawing in black on tracing cloth. (iii) A clear sharp line impression, printed by any process on white or bluish paper. The best results are only obtainable if the drawing is on a larger scale than that required for the copies. Reduction by one-third or by one-half is suitable. Only minor corrections can be carried out at proof stage. The original should be correct and complete.
2. The Vandyke process	Maps, charts, diagrams, and line illustrations, where the highest quality of impression is not essential. Copies can only be reproduced on the same scale as the original. Maximum size, 43″×29″.	One of the following:— 1. A good tracing or drawing in black on tracing cloth 2. Black tracings or drawings on any semi-transparent white or bluish smooth material. Thin, white printing paper is suitable; tracing paper is less so. Drawings on thick paper can be reproduced by this process, but the quality of the results is generally inferior. Corrections are not undertaken and proofs are not usually supplied. The originals should be correct and complete.
3. Lithography ...	Maps and diagrams. Not available for extra-departmental work. Maximum size, 43″×29″.	As the map or diagram has to be redrawn on stone, or on transfer paper for transfer to stone, merely a correct and intelligible pattern is required.
4. Engraving on copper	Maps, line illustrations and diagrams; commissions, addresses, certificates. Not available for extra-departmental work, except in special cases. Maximum size, 40″×27″.	A correct and intelligible pattern is required
5. Photogravure ...	Illustrations or portraits in half-tone ... ... Maximum size, 30″×24″.	One of the following:— 1. The article or object of art which it is proposed to illustrate. 2. A good negative. 3. A good photographic print on paper such as:— Wellington. Kodak. Ensign, glossy bromide. 4. A brush drawing. 5. An oil painting. 6. A good Photographic print on printing out paper. The above are in order of suitability.
6. Half-tone block ...	Illustrations or portraits in half-tone; especially useful when a large number of copies are required, or if the illustration is to be printed as an inset in letter press. The blocks can be set up with type, and are printed in a letter press machine. Maximum size, 20″ × 15″.	The same as for photogravure. The original must be complete and correct as alterations and additions can not be made on the blocks.
7. Line block ...	Small maps, line illustrations or diagrams; especially if a large number of copies are required or which it is required to print as insets in letter press. The blocks can be set up with type, and are printed in a letter press machine. Maximum size, 30″×20″. Above 15″×12″ is not economical.	A clear line drawing or print in black on white paper. The best results are only obtainable if the drawing is on a larger scale than that required for the copies. One-half reduction is suitable. The drawing must be correct and complete as alterations and corrections are extremely difficult and sometimes impossible.

CONTAINED IN SECTION IV.

Whether available for reproduction in colours.	Custody of plates.	REMARKS.
If the copies are required in colours there are two alternatives. 1. The whole of the lettering and detail, irrespective of the colour in which it is to be printed, should be drawn on one "original" in black and a pattern should be supplied indicating the colours in which it is to be reproduced. Flat tints or colour washes can be printed as well as colours in line; no colour must appear on the original. 2. The second method is to prepare a separate 'original' in black for each colour as described under the Vandyke process below.	Plates can be kept standing at a charge of Rs. 10 each, but the Survey of India does not hold itself responsible for their deterioration; ordinarily plates should keep for years. Plates are cleaned off unless a definite request is made for their retention.	This is the ordinary process used in the production of Survey of India Maps. It is more expensive and slower than No. 2, the Vandyke process, but i reduction is employed the results are superior. The quality of the results depends on that of the originals and the degree of reduction employed. Each additional colour in which a job is printed adds considerably to the cost.
A separate trace or drawing is required for black and for each colour. These must be in black irrespective of the colour they refer to and must 'register' exactly with each other. Each of them must show nothing but the lettering and drawing to be printed in the particular colour it refers to. Flat tints or washes of colour can be printed, if they are indicated on a separate colour pattern. No colour must appear on the originals.	The same as for heliozincography, see above	A cheap and rapid process particularly suitable for rough diagrams, maps, plans, &c. The quality of the results depends entirely on that of the original. Each additional colour in which a job is to be printed adds considerably to the cost.
Copies can be printed in colours, a separate stone being drawn for each colour. This adds considerably to the cost.	Stones of extra-departmental jobs are not kept, except in very special cases.	A slow and expensive process practically confined to the production of certain Survey of India Maps.
Copies can be printed in colours if a separate plate is engraved for each colour. This adds considerably to the cost.	Plates can be kept at a charge of Rs. 10 per plate.	This process yields the highest quality of map reproduction. It is, however, very slow and expensive and is confined to the production of certain classes of Survey of India Maps.
Monochrome only ...	Plates are not kept ...	Results are artistic, but the process is a slow and expensive one.
The three-'colour' modification of this process enables coloured originals to be reproduced in colours; within certain limitations all ordinary half-tone blocks are for printing in monochrome only.	The block is the property of the applicant and can be printed at the Survey of India Offices, or by any *good* letter press printer.	A cheap and rapid process as compared with photogravure, but results are less artistic.
A monochrome process not ordinarily used for colours. If colours are required a separate original must be provided for each. These must be in black irrespective of the colours to which they refer. They should show nothing but the lettering and drawing to be printed in each particular colour and must register exactly with each other.	The block is the property of the applicant and can be printed at the Survey of India Offices, or by any *good* letter press printer.	Ordinary maps, line illustrations, and diagrams are more cheaply reproduced by processes 1 or 2.

SECTION V.

Specimens and details of sizes and cost of Printing Papers.

1. The various illustrations given under Section IV are printed on different classes of paper, the class of paper on which each is printed being typed at the head of the page.

2. The following tabular statement gives the papers most generally used with their sizes and cost and the process for which they are suitable:—

THE PRICES GIVEN ARE FOR 500 SHEETS. PROPORTIONATE CHARGES ARE MADE FOR ANY LESS QUANTITY.

Name and description of Paper	Process for which suitable	Double Imperial, 44"×30"			Imperial, 30"×22"			½ Imperial, 22"×15"			¼ Imperial, 15"×11"			⅛ Imperial, 11"×7½"			Double Elephant, 40"×27"			½ Double Elephant, 27"×20"			¼ Double Elephant (Foolscap), 20"×13½"			⅛ Double Elephant (½ Foolscap), 13½"×10"			Reference to Plate showing Specimen Paper. Page.
		Rs.	a.	p.	Rs.	a.	p.	Rs.	a.	p.	Rs.	a.	p.	Rs.	a.	p.	Rs.	a.	p.	Rs.	a.	p.	Rs.	a.	p.	Rs.	a.	p.	
Double Elephant, Proof (thick Bank-Post), 60 lbs.	Photo-zincography	...			...			...			...			...			32	4	0	16	2	0	8	1	0	4	0	6	16
Double Imperial, Litho., 110 lbs.	The Vandyke process	60	0	0	30	0	0	15	0	0	7	8	0	3	12	0	...			...			...			...			17
,, Rag-Litho., 82 lbs.	Lithography, line blocks	49	0	4	24	8	2	12	4	2	6	2	1	3	1	1	...			...			...			...			10, 11, 12
,, Elephant, 67 lbs.		...			...			...			...			...			40	2	5	20	1	2	10	0	7	5	0	8	
,, Imperial, Hollingworth, 150 lbs.	Printing direct from copper.	155	4	0	77	10	0	38	13	0	19	6	6	9	11	3	...			...			...			...			
,, Elephant, Drawing Paper, (Whatman's), 210 lbs.		...			...			...			...			...			444	0	0	222	0	0	111	0	0	...			
,, Elephant, Plate, 185 lbs.	Photogravure	...			...			...			...			...			96	6	0	48	3	0	24	1	6	12	0	9	24, 25, 26
,, ,, 240 lbs.		...			...			...			...			...			80	1	7	40	1	0	20	0	5	10	0	2	

Note.—Photogravure can also be printed on Hollingworth, Bankpost or Litho. paper.

Name and description of Paper	Process for which suitable	Dull Enamelled Chromo, Double Crown.			Double Crown, 30"×20".			½ Double Crown, 20"×15".			¼ Double Crown, 15"×10".			⅛ Double Crown, 10"×7½".			Reference to Plate showing Specimen Paper. Page.
		Rs.	a.	p.	Rs.	a.	p.	Rs.	a.	p.	Rs.	a.	p.	Rs.	a.	p.	
Double Crown, Dull Chromo, Dull Enamelled, 80 lbs.	Half-tone & line blocks.	84	0	0	...			...			...			...			32
Crown, Art, 50 lbs.		...			18	14	9	9	7	5	4	11	8	2	5	11	31
,, ,, 70 lbs.		...			27	6	0	13	11	0	6	13	6	3	6	10	30
,, ,, 90 lbs.		...			35	4	0	17	10	0	8	13	0	4	6	6	29

NOTE.—A percentage of 20% is charged on all classes of paper to cover cost of freight, &c., &c. These charges are included in the prices of papers given in this statement and also in all specimen estimates given in previous pages.

SECTION VI.

Scale of Charges for Work executed at the Photographic and Lithographic Office, Survey of India.

Photographic and Photozincographic Work.

	46¾"×35"	36"×36" and 45"×30"	42"×28"	36"×28"	33"×24"	30"×24"	24"×22"	22"×16" and 20"×15"	15"×12"	12"×10"	10"×8"	8½"×6½"	6½"×4¾"
	Rs. a.	Rs. a.	Rs. a.	Rs. a.	Rs. a.	Rs. a.	Rs. a.	Rs. a.	Rs. a.	Rs. a.	Rs. a.	Rs. a.	Rs. a.
Negatives and Prints—													
Wet Collodion Negatives	30 0	25 0	20 0	17 0	15 0	12 8	8 8	6 0	5 0	4 8	4 0	3 8	......
Dry Plate Negatives	......	......	......	......	......	......	......	......	......	4 8	4 0	3 8	......
Bromide Prints	......	......	......	......	......	2 8	......	3 0	1 8	1 4	0 12	0 8	0 6
Cyanotype Prints	......	......	3 0	......	......	2 8	2 0	1 4	0 12	0 8	0 6	0 4	0 3

Note.—Retouching and correcting Negatives will be charged according to actual cost. Half-tone Negatives and Helio Plates are charged at double the ordinary rates.

	Double Imperial, 44"×30".	Double Elephant, 40"×27".	Imperial, 30"×22".	Foolscap, 20"×13¾".
	Rs. a.	Rs. a.	Rs. a.	Rs. a.
Heliozincography—				
Preparation of plate from a negative (see cost above).	7 0	5 0	4 0	3 0
Proving	7 0	5 0	4 0	3 0
Vandyke Process—				
Preparation of plate	5 0	4 0	3 0	2 0
Proving	7 0	5 0	4 0	3 0

Retouching and correcting plates will be charged according to labour expended plus supervision.

If more than three proofs are required an extra charge will be made.

Proofs are not usually supplied for the Vandyke Process.

Photogravure and Process Work.

		Rs. a.
Photogravure	1 0 per square inch. Minimum	25 0
Half-tone Blocks on Copper—		
A Class	1 0 per square inch. Minimum	6 0
B Class	0 12 ,, ,,	4 0
C Class	0 8 ,, ,,	......
Line Blocks on Zinc—		Rs. a.
A Class	0 8 per square inch. Minimum	3 0
B Class	0 6 ,, ,,	2 8

The rate for printing photogravure plates will be Rs. 10-12-0 per 100 pulls plus cost of paper.

Printing half-tone and line blocks are charged as under :—

	Per 100 pulls.	Per 1,000 pulls.	Making ready.	Typing.
	Rs. a.	Rs. a.	Rs. a.	Rs. a.
One half-tone block	1 0	10 0	3 0	1 0
On line blocks	0 12	7 8	3 0	1 0

Lithographic Work.

	Double Imperial.	Double Elephant.	Imperial.	Foolscap.
	Rs. a.	Rs. a.	Rs. a.	Rs. a.
Transfer to stone	7 0	5 0	4 0	3 0
Proving work on stone	7 0	5 0	4 0	3 0
Hand printing per 25 pulls	6 0	4 0	2 0	1 8
Machine printing first hundred	10 0	6 0	5 0	1 8
Each subsequent hundred up to 1,000	4 0	2 8	2 0	1 0
Each hundred over 1,000	3 0	2 0	1 8	1 0

No rates can be laid down for drawing work, but estimates can always be given when required.

These prices are for printing in one colour only. For maps in more than one colour, the rates charged for each extra printing will be one rupee higher than those given in the table for each hundred of the first 1,000, and eight annas extra for each subsequent 100.

When work is of such a simple nature that it can be given to comparatively unskilled men, the rates for hand printing may be reduced to half those laid down in the table with a minimum of one rupee.

These charges do not include the cost of paper.

APPENDIX.

i.—Indian Army Order No. 506 of 1909.

ii.—Specimen of Indent Form for maps.

INDIA ARMY ORDERS

BY

HIS EXCELLENCY THE COMMANDER-IN-CHIEF IN INDIA.

Army Headquarters, Simla, the 9th December 1912.

728. Training and Manœuvre Regulations,—1909, Indian Supplement.
The following amendment is published for information and will appear in Appendix to India Army Orders, April 1913:—

Chapter III, paragraph 8, is reconstructed as follows:—

"8. Provision of maps.

The following instructions should be followed regarding the purchase of maps for use in connection with training.

1. Since the army in India must be prepared to work in war on ¼-inch maps, the same scale must be used for training in peace, with the one exception referred to in paragraph (3).

2. Standard sheets on the ¼-inch scale are procurable from the Surveyor General, Survey of India, Calcutta, who is prepared to supply them, folded in covers, on the indent of army, division and brigade commanders at a reduced rate of 11 annas a sheet, provided at least one month's notice is given. Applications will only be considered when received from the above mentioned officers.

3. For the normal training in field work of units quartered at defended ports ¼-inch maps will be used. But for the training of the garrisons in their duties in connection with the defence of their ports, the use of larger scale maps (up to one inch) is allowed, when such maps are available.

4. The production of other maps will only be sanctioned under very special circumstances. Applications for such maps should be made to the Chief of the General Staff, and not to the Surveyor General, and should be sent in at least 3 months before the maps are required."

O. 38.

INDENT No.

INDENTS IN DUPLICATE ARE NOT REQUIRED.

Survey of India.

on the MAP RECORD AND ISSUE OFFICE, CALCUTTA, for Maps, &c., required on the public service for the use of the

dated _____ 191 .

Description of Maps.	Scale.	Quantity or number in use or store.	Quantity or number now indented for	Purpose for which required.	Whether required on Government service or whether the cost is to be paid in cash from any Local Fund or other Service.	Cost.	Name of Account Office to which the Bill will be rendered.	How and where to be despatched, and other special Instructions.
						Rs. a.		

I hereby certify that the Maps specified on this Indent are, to the best of my knowledge and belief, and after the most careful examination, indispensably necessary for the purposes set forth.

RECOMMENDED

NOTES.—All charges for maps supplied on the Government service are adjusted by book-debit, in accordance with paragraph 96 of the Civil Account Code.

When mounted maps are required applicants must state clearly how they desire maps to be mounted, e.g., on cloth, on cloth in book form (with dimensions required), varnished or otherwise, or mounted on rollers, &c. Failing particulars, maps will be supplied mounted on cloth only.

Unless it is distinctly stated that maps are required coloured they will be sent uncoloured.

Signature of Indenting Officer.

Countersignature of approving authority.

NOTE.—All Indents for Maps should be forwarded to the Officer in charge Map Record and Issue Office, 13, Wood Street, Calcutta.

Especial attention is requested to the filling up correctly of the last column.

The description and cost of the different Maps, &c., ordinarily kept in store for issue, is given in the Map Catalogue, which may be had on application to the Map Record and Issue Office, for Re. 1.

The mode of transit, and address, or Station to which the Maps are to be consigned, must invariably be specified in full on Indents in the proper column. (Abbreviations lead to mistakes). Indents should not be accompanied with forwarding letters, unless more explanation is necessary than can be given on the face of the Indent.

It is particularly requested that any information which will guide the Map Record and Issue Office in knowing, without further reference, the exact want of the indenting Officer, be put, as far as possible, on face of Indent instead of in covering letters.

All Indents must be duly approved and countersigned by the undermentioned duly authorized officers or by the Secretary to Government under whom indenting Officers may be serving, before they can be supplied, viz:—

Survey of India	by Superintendent, Trigonometrical Surveys, and Circle Superintendents. } or by Surveyor General.
Public Works Department.	,, Superintending Engineers or higher authorities. ,, Superintendent of Works, Famine Relief Circles.
Telegraph Department	,, Provincial Superintendents or higher authorities.
Postal Department	,, Provincial Post Masters General, Deputy Postmasters General, Inspector General, Railway Mail Service, or higher authorities.
Police Department	,, Provincial Inspectors General. ,, Deputy Inspectors General, Commissioner of Police, Calcutta. ,, Superintendents of Police in Bengal and Burma.
Jails	,, Inspector General of Prisons.
Army Department	,, Chief of the General Staff. ,, General Officers Commanding, Northern and Southern Armies. ,, General Officers Commanding Divisions and Brigades and their Brigade Majors. ,, Military Secretary to His Excellency the Commander-in-Chief. ,, Inspector of Coast Defences and Garrison Artillery. ,, Inspector General of Cavalry. ,, Adjutant General and Deputy Adjutants General. ,, Quarter Master General in India. ,, Commandant, Indian Staff College. ,, Director General of Ordnance in India. ,, Director, Army Clothing, Alipore. ,, Commanding Royal Engineers of Divisions or higher authorities. ,, Superintendent, Army Clothing Factory, Madras.
Imperial Service Troops	,, Inspector General.
Accounts Department	,, Comptroller, Auditor General, and Accountants General. ,, Controllers of Military Accounts, Eastern, Northern and Western Circles. ,, Controller of Military Supply and Marine Accounts. ,, Deputy Controllers of Military Accounts in charge of Secunderabad and Burma Divisions.
Marine Department	,, Director and Deputy Director, Royal Indian Marine. ,, Marine Transport Officer, Mandalay. ,, Presidency Port Officer, Madras. ,, Port Officers in Burma.
Medical Department	,, Surgeon General with the Government of India. ,, Administrative Medical Officer, Central Provinces. ,, Sanitary Commissioners, Burma, Punjab and Eastern Bengal and Assam. ,, Principal Medical Officer, His Majesty's Forces. ,, Principal Medical Officers with Local Governments and Administrations. ,, Surgeons General with the Governments of Madras and Bombay.
Political Department	,, Political Agents, or higher authorities.
Criminal Intelligence Department.	,, Director, Criminal Intelligence.
Forest Department	,, Provincial Conservators, and Deputy Conservators of Forests*(1). ,, Officers in charge of Forest Divisions in Burma. ,, Director of the Forest School at Dehra Dun. ,, Officer in charge Forest Map Office, Dehra Dun.
Geological Survey Department.	,, Director, Geological Survey.
Archaeological Survey Department.	,, Director General of Archaeology in India.
Meteorological Department.	,, Meteorological Reporter to the Government of India.
Opium Department	,, Opium Agents.
Educational Department.	,, Directors of Public Instruction.
Revenue Officers	,, Commissioners of Divisions.* (2) ,, Deputy Commissioners and Settlement Officers in Burma. ,, Financial Commissioners, Punjab and Burma. ,, Settlement Commissioners. ,, Commissioner of Northern India Salt Revenue. ,, Commissioners of Excise, Burma, Bengal, Central Provinces and the Punjab. ,, Director of Land Records and Agriculture.
Judicial Officers	,, District and Sessions Judges. ,, Registrars, High Court, United Provinces of Agra and Oudh and Bombay.
Agricultural Department.	,, Agricultural Chemist to the Government of India. ,, Director of Agriculture, Punjab.
Railways	,, Agent and Chief Engineer, Bengal Nagpur Railway. ,, Chief Engineer, Madras and Southern Maharatta Railway. ,, Managers and Chief Engineers, North-Western and Eastern Bengal State Railways.
Miscellaneous	,, Chief Inspector of Mines in India. ,, Reporter on Economic Products to the Government of India. ,, Directors of Survey, Madras, Bengal & Assam, and Bihar & Orissa. ,, Librarian, Imperial Library.
All other Civil Officers or Military Officers in Civil employ.	,, Secretaries to Government or Board of Revenue under which serving.

NOTE.—Includes (1) The Principal Forest Officers in Coorg, the Andamans, and Baluchistan, and (2) the Commissioner of Ajmer-Merwara in Ajmer.

Reg. No. 585, S. I. O.—29-11-13.—500.

INDENT NO.

Memo. of Charges for Map Mounting.

(I)—MOUNTING ON CLOTH—One anna and four pies per square foot.

(II)—MOUNTING ON CLOTH AND FOLDING—One anna and six pies per square foot.

(III)—MOUNTING ON CLOTH IN BOOK FORM OR IN CASE—One anna and six pies per square foot, plus six annas for smaller than foolscap or twelve annas for foolscap or larger size.

(IV)—MOUNTING ON CLOTH AND FEEDING ON ROLLERS AND VARNISHING—One anna and four pies per square foot, plus five annas and six pies per running foot of length of one roller.

N.B.—In the calculation of charges the cost is to be calculated to the nearest whole anna and pies omitted from the total amount.

www.ingramcontent.com/pod-product-compliance
Lightning Source LLC
Chambersburg PA
CBHW081527040426
42447CB00013B/3361